Adult Coloring Book

DRAGONS

Friendly Dragon Prints

Illustrated by MJ Albert

Published by Friendly Dragon Prints
Https://friendlydragonprints.com

- *Coil Bound Coloring Books*
- *Perfect Bound Coloring Books*
- *PDF & PNG Coloring Pages*
- *Journals*
- *Planners*
- *Stickers*
- *Cards*

Practice - Check your colors on a test image and/or color chart swatch page.

Protection Sheet - Place a sheet of thick paper behind the page you are working on to protect the next image and/or table surface.

PRINT - Printing onto high quality artist paper is a popular way to get the most out of a coloring design purchase. The following are my recommendations:

Colored Paper - For those who don't enjoy coloring on a plain white page, colored paper is the answer. I truly love Stonehenge colored papers for pencils. It has a very nice tooth and accepts multiple layers beautifully. My Epson WF 3750 accepts this paper weight with no issues.

White Paper for Pencils - Springhill Vellum Bristol White 67lb Cover - This paper has a nice thickness and tooth for colored pencil work. Check to make sure that your printer will print onto card stock.

White Paper for Markers - Canson Bristol Smooth or Bee Artist Marker. Mixed media paper is nice if you want to use both markers and colored pencils but note that the tooth will use a lot of ink and can wear down your markers. Card stock thickness can be an issue for some printers. A flat feed printer works best.

Friendlydragonsprints.com

ISBN: 978-1-79484-424-7

Copyright 2020 MJ Albert - All Rights Reserved

Published by Friendly Dragon Prints

Idaho USA

Published by Friendly Dragon Prints

Idaho USA

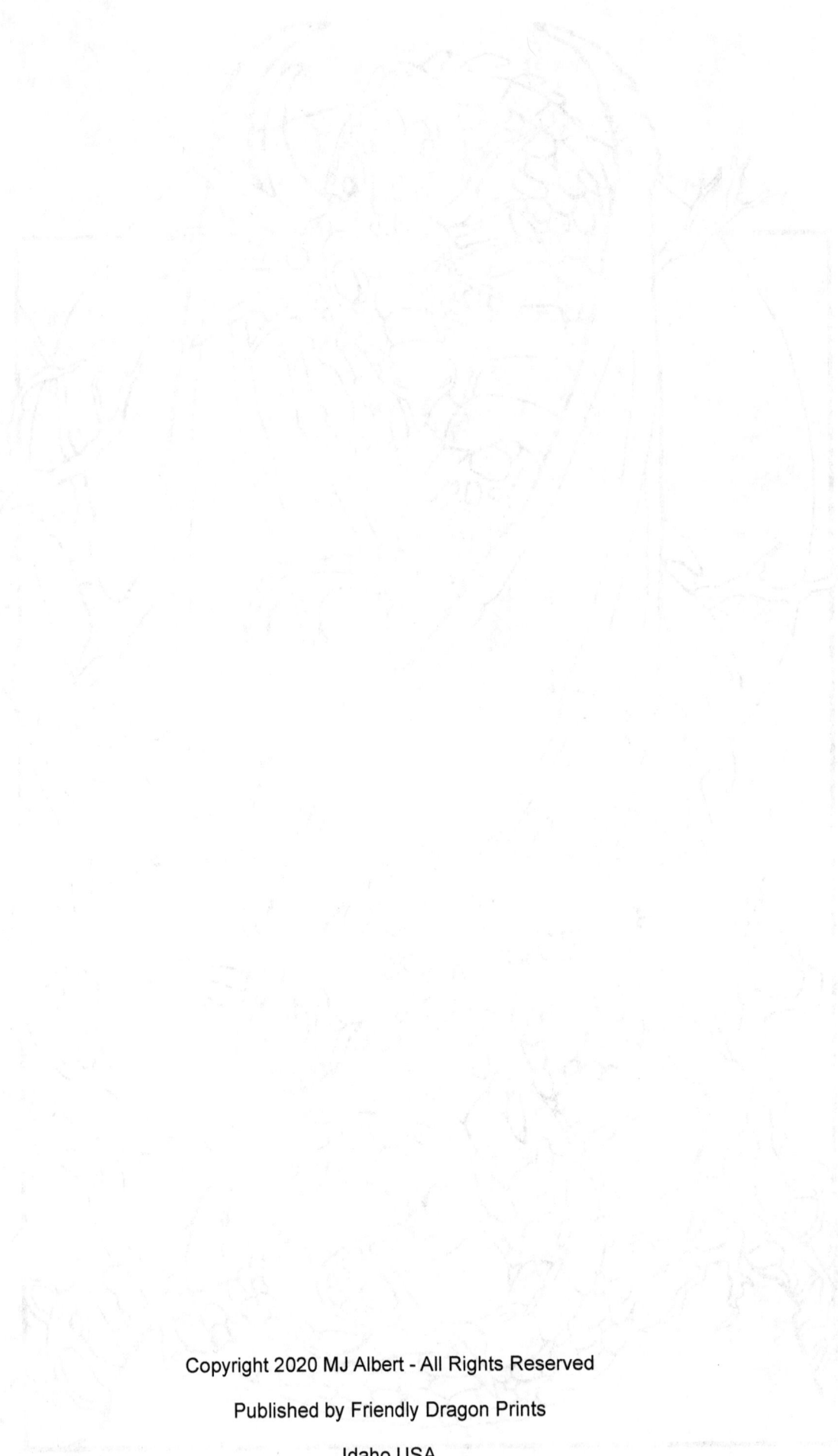

Published by Friendly Dragon Prints

Idaho USA

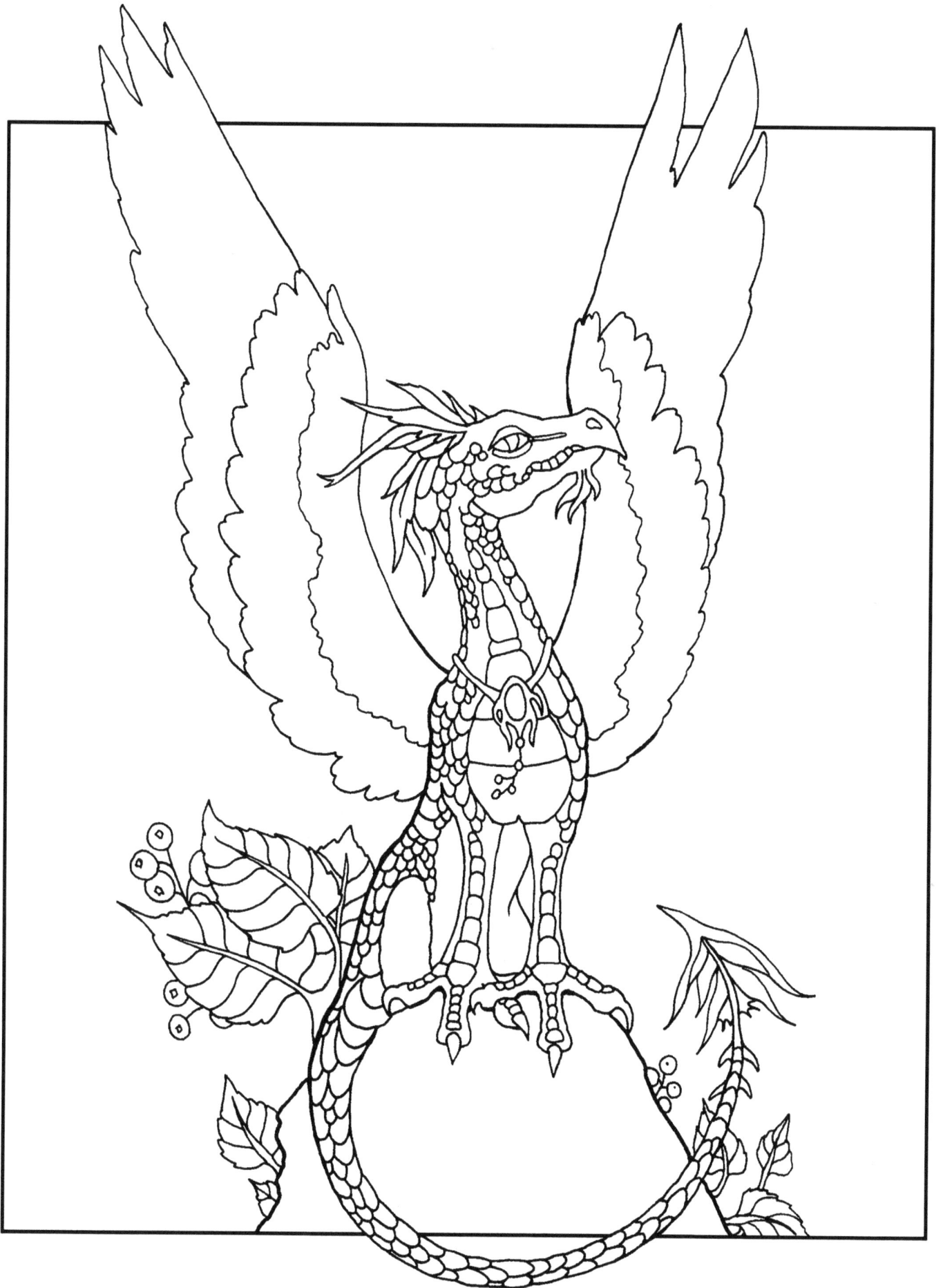

Published by Friendly Dragon Prints

Idaho USA

Published by Friendly Dragon Prints

Idaho USA

Published by Friendly Dragon Prints

Idaho USA

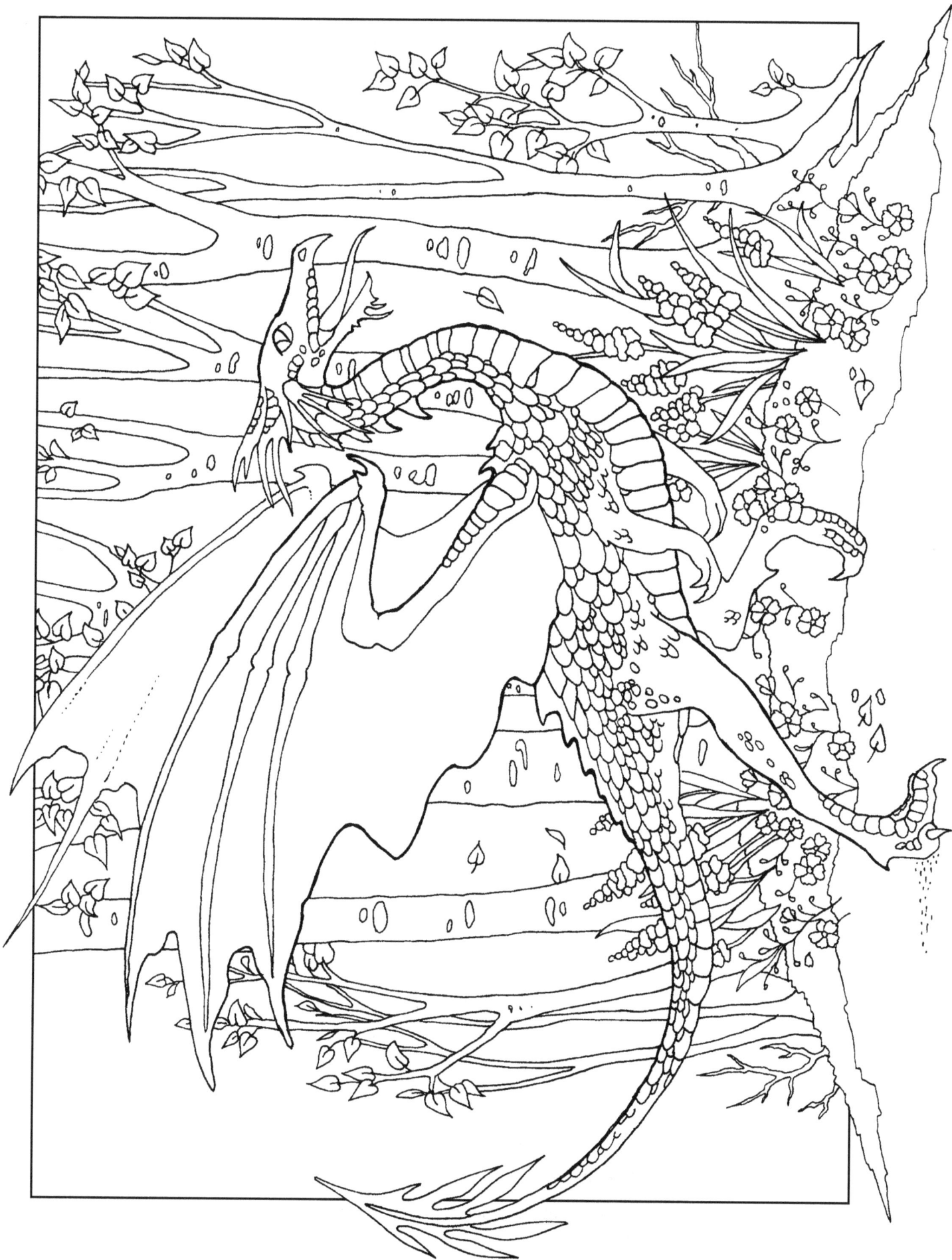

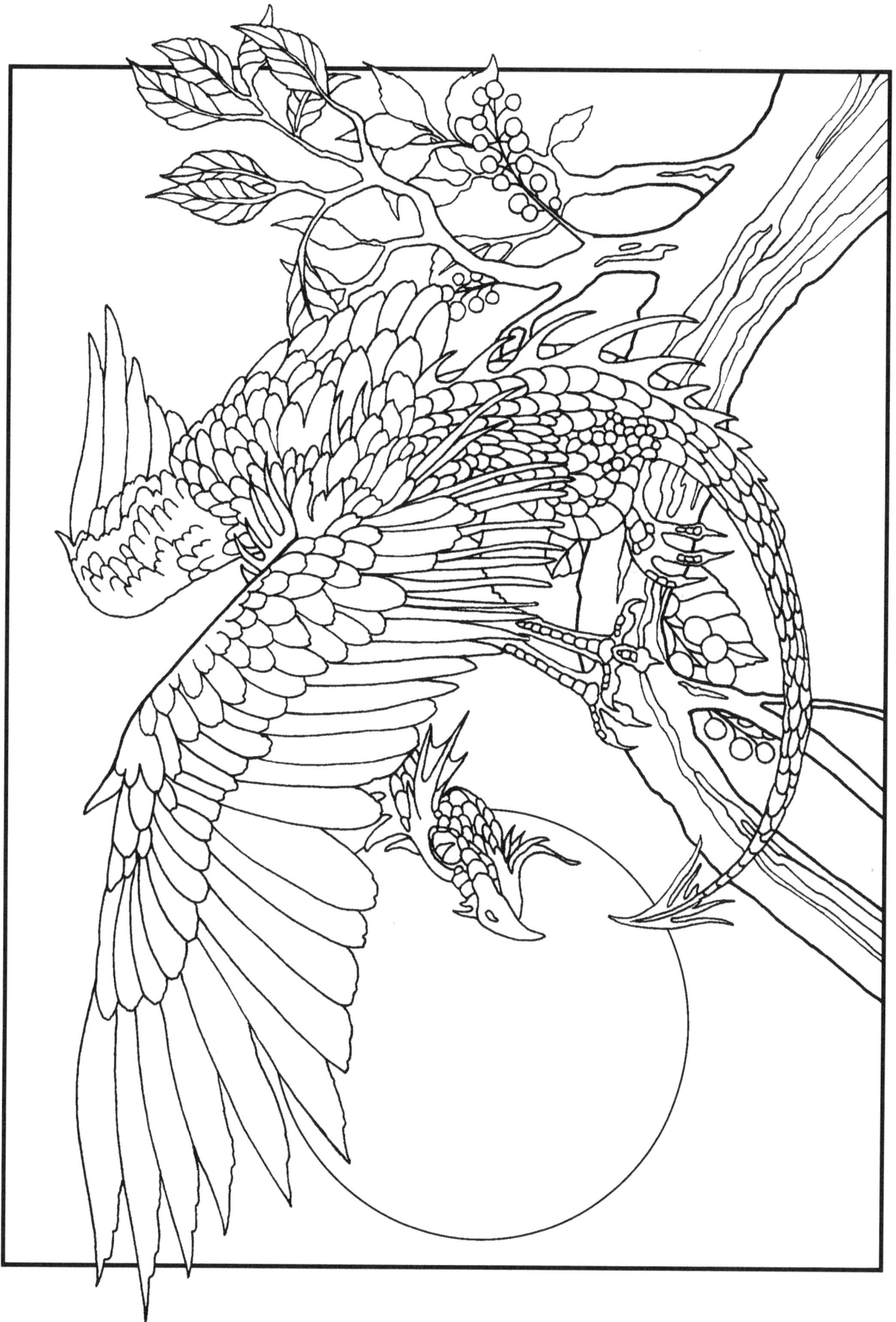

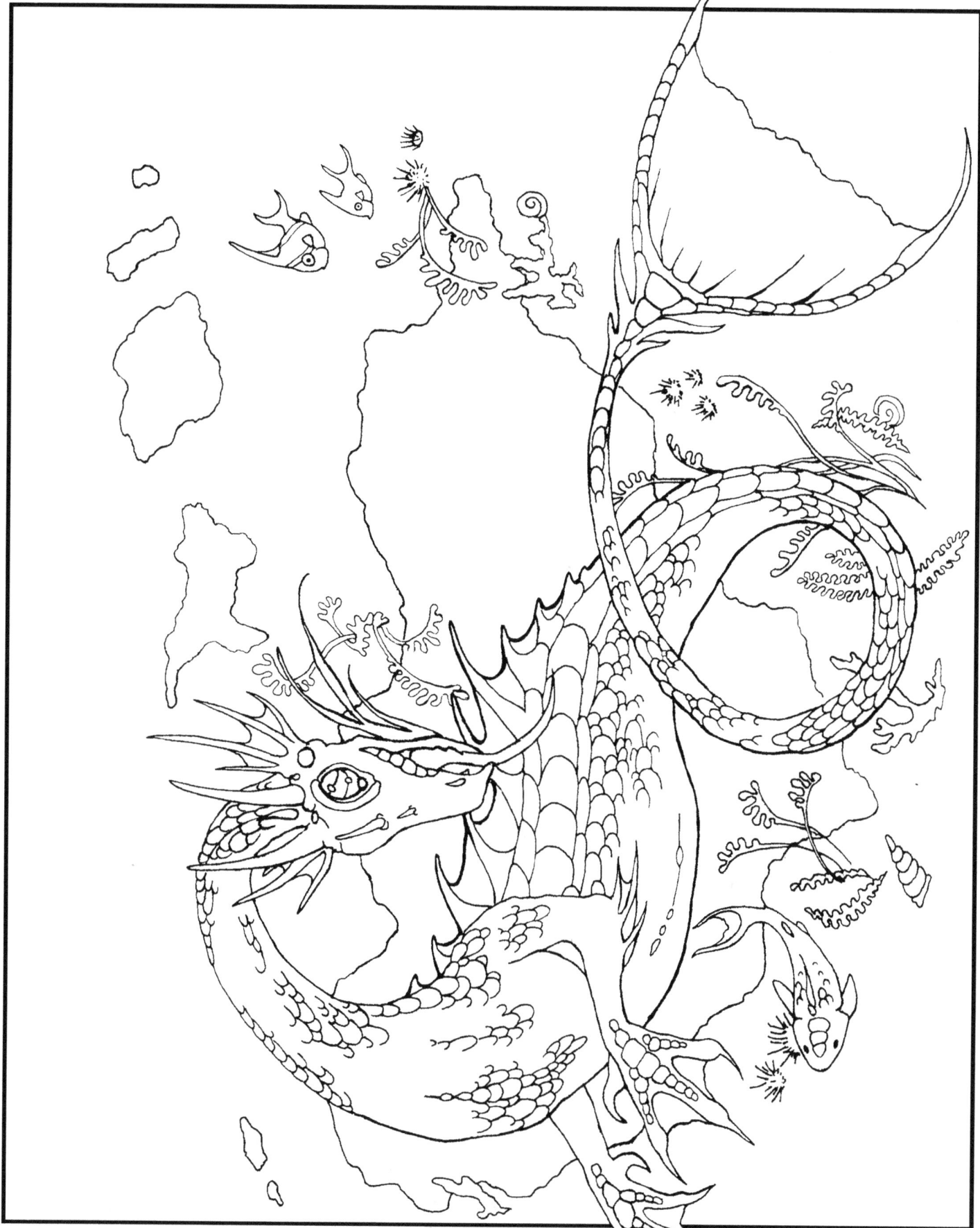

Published by Friendly Dragon Prints

Idaho USA

Published by Friendly Dragon Prints

Idaho USA

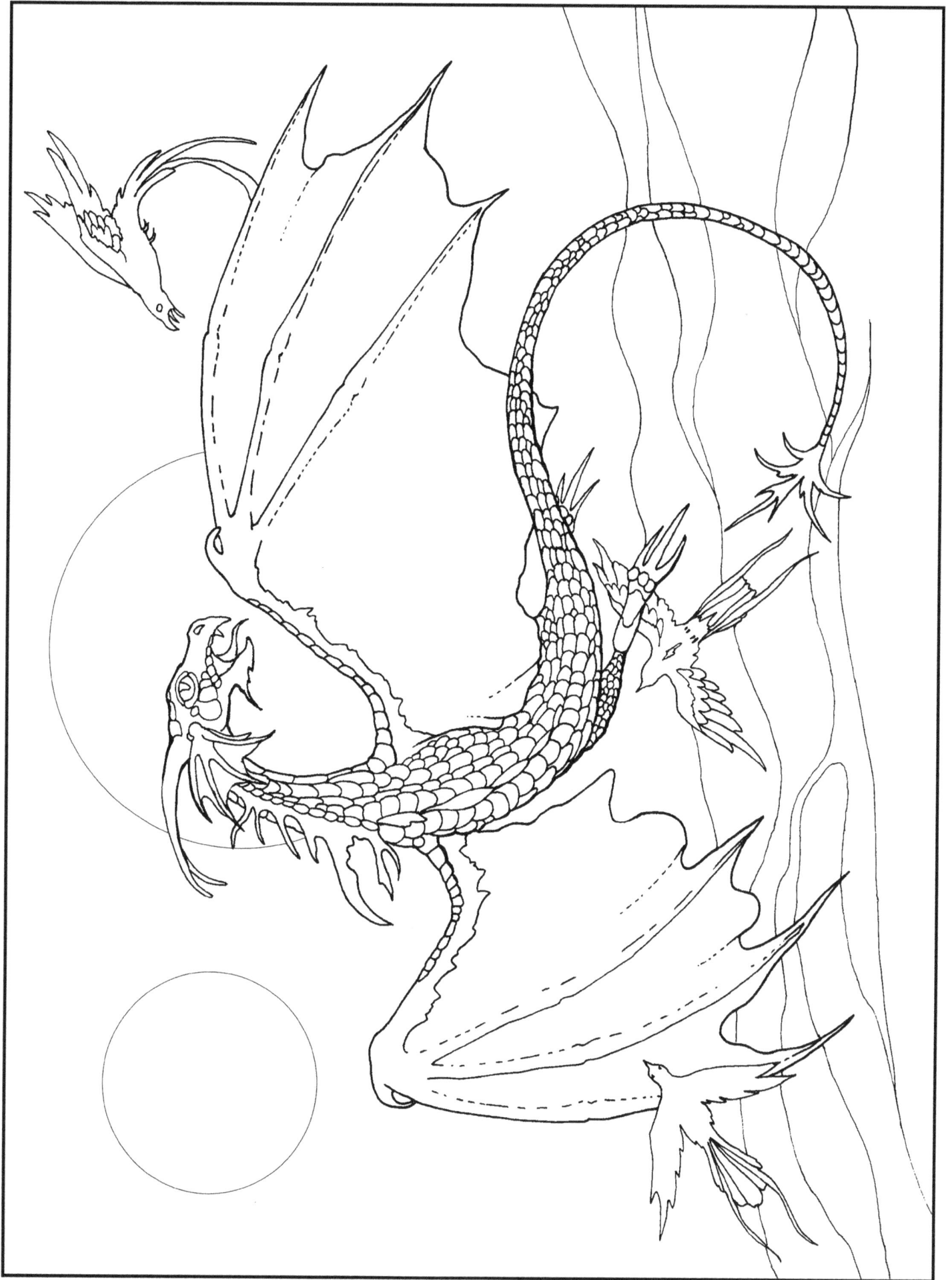

Published by Friendly Dragon Prints

Idaho USA

Published by Friendly Dragon Prints

Idaho USA

Published by Friendly Dragon Prints

Idaho USA

Published by Friendly Dragon Prints

Idaho USA

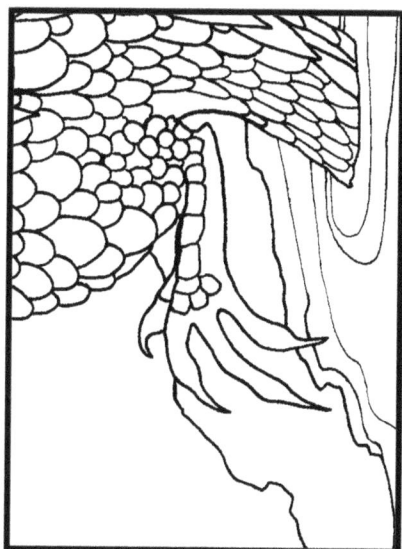

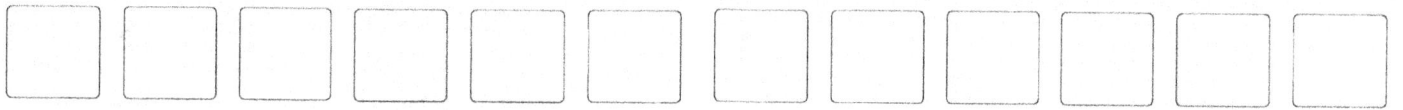

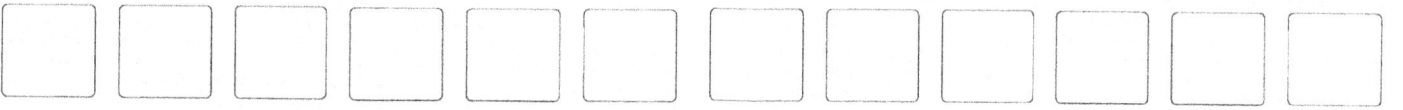

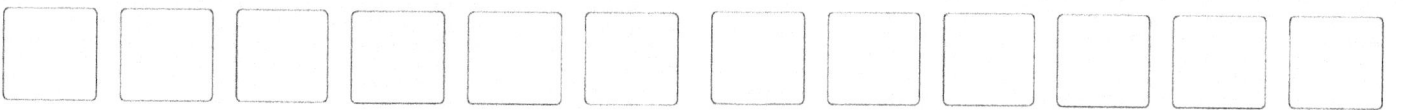

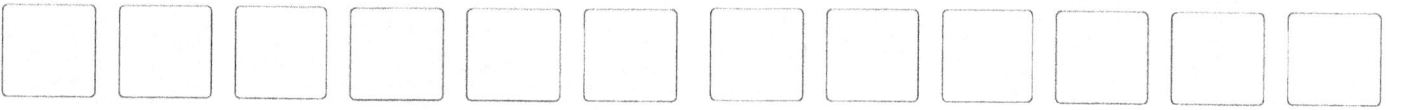

www.ingramcontent.com/pod-product-compliance
Lightning Source LLC
Chambersburg PA
CBHW081547040426
42448CB00015B/3247